To Alissa

Christmas 90

Love, Monita + Dave.

Nature's Footprints

IN THE
FOREST

By Q. L. Pearce and W. J. Pearce

Illustrated by Delana Bettoli

Silver Press

For my brother
Phillip
—D.B.

10   9   8   7   6   5   4   3   2   1

Library of Congress Cataloging-in-Publication Data

Pearce, Q.L. (Querida Lee) Nature's footprints in the forest / text by Q.L. Pearce and W.J. Pearce ; pictures by Delana Bettoli. p.   cm. Summary: The reader is invited to follow animal tracks and observe the habits and habitat of several forest animals. 1. Forest fauna—Juvenile literature.   [1. Forest animals. 2. Animals—Habits and behavior.]   I. Pearce, W. J.   II. Bettoli, Delana, ill.   III. Title.
QL112.P43   1990
599—dc20
89-39509
CIP
AC
ISBN 0-671-68830-8   ISBN 0-671-68826-X (lib. bdg.)

A Note to Parents

NATURE'S FOOTPRINTS is a read-aloud picture book series that introduces children to a wide variety of animals in a unique, interactive way.

Ten animals are presented in pairs, along with a sample of each animal's footprints. In the scene that follows, the animals can be found by tracking the paths of their footprints, thereby building your child's observational skill in a lively, fun format.

Detailed illustrations and text provide more information about the animals. Encourage your child to point out details about the animals and their environment.

Accompanying the NATURE'S FOOTPRINTS series is the NATURE'S FOOTPRINTS FIELD GUIDE—a handy, colorful reference guide that teaches children even more about the animals in this series.

THE BEAVER

The beaver lives in a stream.

It builds a home of mud and branches.

The beaver's home is warm and dry inside.

THE FROG

The frog lives near a pond.

It lives among the leaves and mud.

Baby frogs called tadpoles live in the water.

The beaver cuts tree branches with its sharp teeth.

Follow nature's footprints.

They will lead you to the busy beaver.

The frog eats insects and fish.

Follow nature's footprints.

They will lead you to the jumping frog.

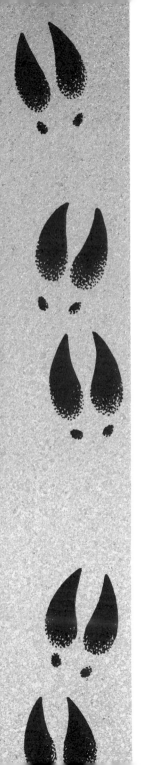

THE DEER

The deer eats leaves and grass in its forest home.

A male deer is called a buck.

A female deer is called a doe.

THE RED FOX

The red fox lives in a burrow in the ground.

The fox's burrow is called a den.

The den is lined with the fox's soft hair.

The deer hides among the trees and bushes.

Follow nature's footprints.

They will lead you to the hidden deer.

The fox has a special hiding place, too.

Follow nature's footprints.

They will lead you to a secret passageway.

THE RABBIT

Some rabbits live together in a warren.

A warren is a group of underground burrows.

Other rabbits dig shallow nests on top of the ground.

THE BEAR

The bear lives in a den.

The den may be under a fallen tree or on a rocky ledge.

The bear usually sleeps in its den for much of the winter.

Baby rabbits are called kittens.

Follow nature's footprints.

They will lead you to the playful kitten.

Baby bears are called cubs.

Follow nature's footprints.

They will lead you to the curious cub.

THE WOODPECKER

Rat-ta-tat-ta-tat-ta-tat!

The woodpecker drills a nest hole in a dead tree.

It lines the hole with wood chips and bark.

THE RACCOON

The raccoon may live in a hollow tree or under a log.

It rests in its home most of the day.

Then the raccoon waddles out to search for food at night.

The woodpecker pecks the tree bark looking for insects to eat.

Follow nature's footprints.

They will lead you to the hungry woodpecker.

The raccoon often rinses its food before it eats.

Follow nature's footprints.

They will lead you to the smart raccoon.

THE OWL

Hoo! Hoo! The owl calls out from high in a tree.

The owl may live in a hollow tree trunk or on a rocky ledge.

Sometimes the owl moves into an old nest left by

another large bird.

THE SKUNK

The skunk makes its home in an underground burrow.
It doesn't mind sharing its burrow with other animals.
Sometimes the skunk moves into an old burrow left by
another animal.

The owl is hard to see in the shadows of the moonlit night.

Follow nature's footprints.

They will lead you to the hidden owl.

Like many forest animals, the skunk searches for food at night.

Follow nature's footprints.

They will lead you to the hungry skunk.